THE HAPPY BEANS 'BEST GR. JO

"Remember we love from the heart, we give from the heart so we must treasure it."

JACQUELINE MERNE

Copyright © 2018 Jacqueline Merne

Published by DVG STAR PUBLISHING

All rights reserved.

ISBN: 1-912547-18-X
ISBN-13: 978-1-912547-18-0

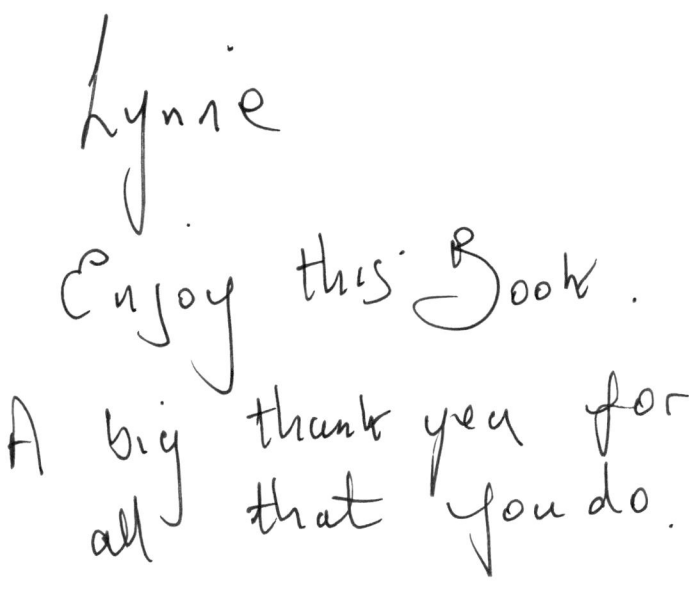

DEDICATED TO

The Hope Foundation and everyone who has come into my life at various times, you have shown me the true meaning of gratitude.

With Gratitude and Thanks to

My family and friends who have supported me every step of the way.

Professor Chris Imafidon for his ongoing support. Philip Chan for all his help and encouragement and for introducing me to Mayooran Senthilmani of DVG STAR Publishing. Visualarts for providing the cover graphics along with Galih Windu for my 'Happy BEANS' Characters.

My husband Gerry, my rock, for his ongoing loving support.

You have all brought a ray of sunshine into my life.

CONTENTS

About the Hope Foundation 1

Introduction to Giving Gratitude 7

My Top 9 Steps 10

Gratitude Journal 17

My 3R Rule 204

About the Author 205

"There are many injustices in this world, but few as harsh as a child's future stolen; life over before it has even begun. It should never hurt to be a child. Support HOPE in the fight for street and slum children's human rights."

Maureen Forrest, Hon. Director, The Hope Foundation

"To see first-hand how people who have virtually nothing at all show so much gratitude for the simplest of things has etched a place in my heart and enriched my life forever. I truly believe this has opened my eyes to a life filled with joy, happiness and true contentment. With gratitude and thanks to the Hope Foundation for giving me the opportunity to be part of this empowering effort."

Jacqueline Merne, Hope Volunteer - Ireland, UK & India

BUILDING FUTURES – CHANGING LIVES

HOPE is dedicated to promoting the protection of street and slum children primarily in Kolkata (Calcutta), and the most underprivileged in India, to promote immediate and lasting change in their lives.

ABOUT THE HOPE FOUNDATION

It is estimated that up to 250,000 children go to sleep each night on the streets and in the slums of Kolkata, hungry and without shelter or protection. The Hope Foundation (HOPE) was established in 1999 by Irish humanitarian, Maureen Forest, to improve the lives of these children.

Since HOPE began, they have extended their support to their communities and now provide a holistic approach to development and work with Kolkata's most vulnerable inhabitants, namely street and slum dwelling children and adults. HOPE is currently reaching out to tens of thousands of people each year through their projects. HOPE have offices based in Cork, Dublin, the UK, and India and work with 9 local Indian NGOs on the ground in Calcutta, now known as Kolkata.

WHAT HOPE DO

HOPE work with committed, passionate people and local NGOs in Kolkata to change the lives of the most underprivileged people in the world today. They never regard the foundation as a charity but as an organization that invests in the sustainability of human life, affording people with necessary skills an opportunity to become self-sufficient.

HOPE provides funding and support to over **60 projects** on the ground in Kolkata which include.

Protection	Life Skills & Vocational Training
Healthcare & Nutrition	Awareness & Capacity Building
Education	Emergency Response

HOW YOU CAN HELP

- Donate online

- Sponsor a child's education

- Give a Gift of HOPE

- Organise a fundraising event

- Volunteer at home or in Kolkata

- Take part in the HOPE Himalayan Walk, Paint, Yoga or Street Photography adventures in India

- Leave a Legacy

- Become a corporate partner

- Get your Local school involved

IT SHOULD NEVER HURT TO BE A CHILD

The Hope Foundation works to build futures and change lives of street connected children in Kolkata, India, Founded by Maureen Forrest in 1998.

HOPE provides sustainable holistic solutions to child protection and development in Kolkata.

This is achieved through our education programmes, healthcare programmes, including our own HOPE Hospital, vocational training centre, protection homes and emergency response.

There are many ways to engage and help HOPE to continue our work in Kolkata:

- Corporate fundraising - great team building and volunteering opportunities
- CSR either as corporate charity or via employee matching programmes
- Volunteering in Kolkata
- Championing one of our many projects
- Sponsoring a child

To find out more you can contact HOPE in:

Ireland www.hopefoundation.ie
         office@hopefoundation.ie
UK   www.thehopefoundation.org.uk
         info@thehopefoundation.org.uk
India   www.hopechild.org
         info@hopechild.org

"Jacqueline is a world class coach and consultant – and one with a huge advantage over so many practitioners….. she's been there and got the T-shirt!! I've grown to rate and respect her skills and advice. I think it was President J F Kennedy who said "the time to fix the roof is before the storm". The same applies to our own personal situations".

Kim Rawson, International business leader on both sides of the Atlantic.

"Gratitude, like oxygen gives us our life force"

Jacqueline Merne

Introduction to Giving Gratitude

"Connect… Connect…Connect deeper…deeper and even deeper still… Make love your reason, Gratitude your song, Joy your motivation and Paying it Forward your way of life."

Sabrina Ben Salmi

There are many definitions of gratitude. I like the definition from the Harvard Business School which says that gratitude is: -

"a thankful appreciation for what an individual receives, whether tangible or intangible. With gratitude, people acknowledge the goodness in their lives…. As a result, gratitude also helps people connect to something larger than themselves as individuals – whether to other people, nature, or a higher power"

Gratitude costs absolutely nothing to practice and can be practiced in any setting of daily life, from our homes to our schools and in our workplace. Practicing gratitude is such a powerful tool to help increase your personal wellbeing and happiness.

Writing a Gratitude Journal is a very positive and uplifting exercise. At the beginning it takes a bit of practice to remember to do it. Jotting down all the things you are grateful for can have an enormous positive impact on how you feel inside. If you want to achieve the most benefit from your journal you must write about what you are grateful for in detail. The secret to your success is that all your gratitude entries must be specific. There is little or no point in writing down lists of things for the sake of it. You must feel the emotion as you write and really feel what you are thankful for. This is very powerful and will pay real dividends.

Since starting my own gratitude journal I definitely experience more joy in my life. I am now attuned to, and have become more appreciative of the simpler things in life. It has ensured that I experience many precious moments whereas previously they might have gone unnoticed. As you make this a habit it can be the best part of any day and a pleasure to do. I like to write it the old fashioned way and put pen to paper however, if you prefer and find it handier to do it all digitally that's perfect too.

When you get into this daily practice you soon uncover personal insights about yourself which can really help you unravel any negative traits you may have, and as we know we all have some. If you ever have an off day, as we all do from time to time, having gratitude can work its magical powers and you can look back and see all the happy thoughts and great memories you have jotted down. You might even catch yourself smiling!

Psychologist Professor Robert Emmons, from the University of California, says:

"In our studies we ask people to keep gratitude journals for just three weeks and the results have been overwhelming. We've studied more than a thousand people, from ages eight to eighty, and found that people who practice gratitude consistently report a host of benefits:

- More joy, optimism, and happiness
- Higher levels of positive emotions
- Better sleep
- Less anxiety and depression

- Increased self-esteem
- Less stress and reduced negativity
- Acting with more generosity and compassion
- Feeling less lonely and isolated
- Stronger immune system and lower blood pressure
- Fewer symptoms of illness

The reason for this, says Prof Emmons, is that by taking the time to write down what we are thankful for forces us to celebrate the present, gives us a higher sense of self-worth, blocks negative emotions and builds up a resistance to stress."

According to Oprah Winfrey if you allow yourself to feel gratitude in the present moment, in the now, what she promises is that the spiritual dimension of your life begins to change. It opens up and expands and you just grow with it. If you want to change your state of being start to be grateful.

"Be thankful for what you have, you'll end up having more. If you concentrate on what you don't have you'll never, ever have enough."

Oprah Winfrey

My Top 9 Steps

Here are My top 9 Steps that will guide you in starting your own Gratitude Diary.

1 Simply be Grateful

Tune into your daily life and be watchful for all the good things that unfold.

2 Don't wait. Start Today

I like to write at night as it helps me to gather my thoughts and gives me a sense of calm before I go to sleep.

If you find it helpful to write as you think of what you are grateful for throughout the day that's good too.

Others find writing at the start of the day sets them up with a positive flow to their day.

There is no right way, do whatever works best for you – go for it.

3 Write with Emotion

Don't scribble a long list to have something done quickly. It's more important to write a few things with genuine belief and feeling.

4 Focus on You

Be grateful for being you and your ability to function. For example – are you artistic, can you paint, knit, make clothes, sing, dance or play an instrument? Are you good at languages? Are you a good listener? I'll bet when you give it some thought you will surprise yourself in what talents you have already. Describe and appreciate your talents, skills and accomplishments. Some you may have forgotten about. Simply be grateful for all you have. Be aware of all you can do and experience with your gifts, the gift of life itself.

5 Write in the Positive

Keep any negative thoughts out of your journal. By doing this you will soon find positivity is so powerful and overrides the negativity.

6 Who are all the People you Care About?

Focus on and be grateful for the people in your life over the possessions you have. Include your family and friends. Write down all the positive things you feel about them. Why are you grateful for them? There is power in words so write it down. Perhaps there are others in your life you may not be too enamored with. Search for their good points. This can help you as you see there is good in everyone. You may see them in a different light which can be uplifting. Make space for some photos of family and friends in your journal.

7 Be Creative in your Thinking

Be open minded and practice awareness in your day to day life. Again you may be surprised with all the positivity around you that you never gave any thought to previously.

8 Write about your Daily Experiences

Write about happy times and daily encounters with people in passing, good deeds you might do for others and others might do for you. Who did you share time with or meet for a coffee? Be thankful for your leisure time, any work interactions, the community in general. It can be a fulfilling experience to jot it down with feeling and see it in print

9 Pleasant Surprises

See your life as a gift and savor those unexpected pleasant surprises as these can elicit far stronger levels of gratitude.

From my own experiences of journaling I find it more fulfilling not to rush through this exercise as if it is just another item on my to-do list. The important thing to remember is that your journal is personal to you and you can write your own experiences as you see, feel, hear and touch them.

THE HAPPY BEANS 'BEST DAY EVER' JOURNAL

Keep writing, at least give it a fair chance. It's a matter of getting into the habit. It takes at least 21 days to create a habit. So I would urge you to keep in the positive flow, and see for yourself what unfolds for you. Remember positivity attracts positivity. When you make this practice part of your day you will soon reap the benefits and rewards. Our lives become richer and more colourful. You will in turn experience more pleasure and enjoyment from the simplest of things in life.

> *"Gratitude and attitude are not challenges, they are choices."*
>
> **Robert Braathe**

Gratitude Journal

Add your own family and friends picture here

> *"Be in love with the world – Smile more."*
>
> *Jacqueline Merne*

Gratitude Journal

> *"Gratitude is the Single most important ingredient to living a successful and fulfilled life."*
>
> Jack Canfield

Gratitude Journal

> "Don't count the days,
> Make the
> day count."

Muhammad Ali

Gratitude Journal

> *"One of the greatest gifts you can give someone is thanking them for being part of your life."*
>
> Unknown

Gratitude Journal

> *"The real gift of gratitude - The more grateful you are, the more present you become."*
>
> Robert Holden

Gratitude Journal

"Count your blessings – Be grateful for each day and invite sunshine into your world."

Jacqueline Merne

Gratitude Journal

"It's not the joy that makes us grateful, its gratitude that makes us joyful."

Brother David Steindl-Rast

Gratitude Journal

> *"When you realize nothing is lacking the whole world belongs to you."*
>
> *Lao Tzu*

Gratitude Journal

> "When you change the way you look at things, the things you look at change."
>
> Wayne Dyer

Gratitude Journal

> *"When you practice gratefulness, there is a sense of respect for others."*
>
> **The Dalai Lama**

Gratitude Journal

_____

_____

_____

_____

_____

_____

_____

_____

_____

_____

_____

_____

_____

_____

_____

_____

_____

_____

> "There is something magical about everyday …You have to seek it."
>
> Jacqueline Merne

Gratitude Journal

"Feeling gratitude and not expressing it is like wrapping a present and not giving it."

William Arthur Ward

Gratitude Journal

> "Gratitude opens the door to the power, the wisdom, the creativity of the universe; you open the door through gratitude."
>
> *Deepak Chopra*

Gratitude Journal

> *"Gratitude is Riches, Complaint is Poverty."*
>
> *Doris Day*

Gratitude Journal

"Giving Gratitude Elevates our Mood and Fills our Heart with Joy."

Jacqueline Merne

Gratitude Journal

_____
_____
_____
_____
_____
_____
_____
_____

Use this space to be creative

"Let us not look back in anger, nor forward in fear, but around in awareness."

James Thurber

Gratitude Journal

"Gratitude is an art of painting an adversity into a lovely picture."

Kak Sri

Gratitude Journal

> *"Change your expectations for appreciation and the world changes instantly."*
>
> *Tony Robbins*

Gratitude Journal

> *"Be grateful for a digital detox, simply unplug switch your mind off and relax."*
>
> *Jacqueline Merne*

Gratitude Journal

> *"Gratitude is not the result of things that happen to us, it is an attitude we cultivate by practice."*
>
> *Alan Cohen*

Gratitude Journal

> *"Opportunities, relationships, even money flowed my way when I learned to be grateful no matter what happened in my life."*
>
> *Oprah Winfrey*

Gratitude Journal

> *"Gratitude helps us to see what is there and what isn't."*
>
> *Annette Bridges*

Gratitude Journal

"*A simple 'thank you' can lift the spirit and elevate the mood.*"

Jacqueline Merne

Gratitude Journal

> *"Give gratitude for the power of hearing. Listen or your tongue will keep you deaf."*
>
> **Native American Proverb**

Gratitude Journal

> *"Don't undervalue the near when aiming at the far."*
>
> *Euripides*

Gratitude Journal

_____
_____
_____
_____
_____
_____
_____
_____
_____

Use this space to be creative

"It's not what you gather but what you scatter that tells what kind of life you have lived."

Helen Walton

Gratitude Journal

> "To experience true happiness is to be in the flow of gratitude."
>
> Jacqueline Merne

Gratitude Journal

"No gesture is too small when done with gratitude."

Oprah Winfrey

Gratitude Journal

> *"The miracle of gratitude is that it shifts your perception to such an extent that it changes the world you see."*
>
> *Dr. Robert Holden*

Gratitude Journal

> "Gratitude unlocks the fullness of life. It turns what we have into enough. And more. It turns denial into acceptance, chaos to order, confusion to clarity."
>
> *Melody Beattie*

Gratitude Journal

> *"You can have everything in life you want, if you will just help other people get what they want."*
>
> *Zig Ziglar*

Gratitude Journal

> "We often take for granted the very things that most deserve our gratitude."
>
> Cynthia Ozick

Gratitude Journal

> *"Your experience of life is not based on your life but on what you pay attention to."*
>
> Gregg Krech

Gratitude Journal

> *"Do not take anything for granted not one smile or one breath, or one night in your cozy bed."*
>
> **Terry Guillemets**

Gratitude Journal

"When we focus on our gratitude, the tide of disappointment goes out and the tide of love rushes in."

Kristin Armstrong

Gratitude Journal

_____
_____
_____
_____
_____
_____
_____
_____
_____

Use this space to be creative

> *"Gratitude is not only the greatest of virtues, but the parent of all others."*
>
> *Marcus Tullius Cicero*

Gratitude Journal

"Gratitude brings warmth to the giver and the receiver alike."

Robert D. Hales

Gratitude Journal

"Focus and pay attention to all you have and you will appreciate its true value."

Jacqueline Merne

Gratitude Journal

> *"Gratitude unlocks the fullness of life. It turns what we have into enough, and more. It can turn a meal into a feast, a house into a home, a stranger into a friend."*
>
> *Melody Beattie*

Gratitude Journal

"Gratitude is one of the most medicinal emotions we can feel. It elevates our moods and fills us with joy."

Sara Avant Stover – 'The Way of the Happy Woman'

Gratitude Journal

THE HAPPY BEANS 'BEST DAY EVER' JOURNAL

> *"Today's gratitude buys tomorrow's happiness."*
>
> *Michael McMillian*

Gratitude Journal

> *"Giving gratitude can make what seems like a complicated life…So simple."*
>
> *Jacqueline Merne*

Gratitude Journal

> *"One of the secrets of a long and fruitful life is to forgive everybody, everything, every night before you go to bed."*
>
> **Bernard M. Baruch**

Gratitude Journal

> *"What can you do to promote world peace? Go home and love your family."*
>
> *Mother Teresa*

Gratitude Journal

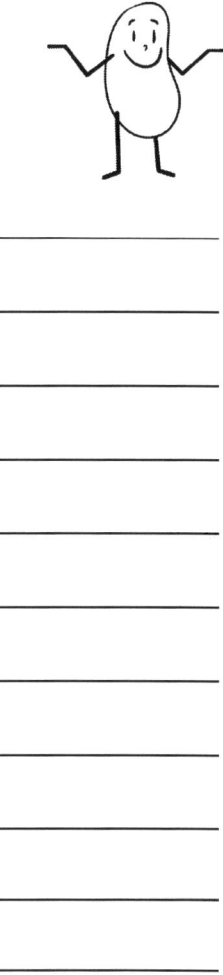

> "Think positive and positivity will flow."

Jacqueline Merne

Gratitude Journal

Use this space to be creative

"The purpose of life is a life of purpose."

Robert Byrne

Gratitude Journal

"Don't ask what the world needs. Ask what makes you come alive and then go and do that, because what the world needs is people who have come alive."

Howard Martin

Gratitude Journal

> *"God gave you a gift of 86,400 seconds today. Have you used one to say Thank You."*
>
> *William Arthur Ward*

Gratitude Journal

> *"Be inspired by the simple things in life, breath the wonder of nature into your day."*
>
> *Jacqueline Merne*

Gratitude Journal

> *"The deepest craving of human nature is the need to be appreciated."*
>
> **William James**

Gratitude Journal

THE HAPPY BEANS 'BEST DAY EVER' JOURNAL

> *"Off with you! You're a happy fellow, for you'll give happiness and joy to many other people. There is nothing greater or better than that!"*
>
> *Ludwig van Beethoven*

Gratitude Journal

> "He is a wise man who does not grieve for the things for which he has not, but rejoices for those which he has."
>
> *Epictetus*

Gratitude Journal

> *"I am happy and grateful for being me."*
>
> *Jacqueline Merne*

Gratitude Journal

> *"Things turn out the best for people who make the best of the way things turn out."*
>
> *John Wooden*

Gratitude Journal

"*Praise the bridge that carried you over.*"

George Colman

Gratitude Journal

_____
_____
_____
_____
_____
_____
_____
_____
_____
_____

Use this space to be creative

> *"You cannot do a kindness too soon because you never know how soon it will be too late."*
>
> *Ralph Waldo Emerson*

Gratitude Journal

> "Feel the love all around you and fill your heart with joy."
>
> Jacqueline Merne

Gratitude Journal

"Gratitude is a currency that we can mint for ourselves, and spend without fear of bankruptcy."

Fred De Witt Van Amburgh

Gratitude Journal

"If you count all your assets, you always show a profit."

Robert Brault

Gratitude Journal

> "We can only be said to be alive in those moments when our hearts are conscious of our treasures."
>
> Thornton Wilder

Gratitude Journal

"No one who achieves success does so without the help of others. The wise and confident acknowledge this help with gratitude."

Alfred North Whitehead

Gratitude Journal

"The only people with whom you should try to get even are those who have helped you."

John E. Southard

Gratitude Journal

> *"When I started counting my blessings my whole life turned around."*
>
> *Willie Nelson*

Gratitude Journal

"Forget yesterday – it has already forgotten you. Don't sweat tomorrow – you haven't even met. Instead open your eyes and your heart to a truly precious gift – today."

Steve Maraboli

Gratitude Journal

"Be in love with the world – Smile more."

Jacqueline Merne

Gratitude Journal

_____
_____
_____
_____
_____
_____
_____
_____
_____

Use this space to be creative

> "At times, our light goes out and is rekindled by a spark from another person. Each of us has caused to think with deep gratitude of those who have lightened the flame within us."
>
> Albert Schweitzer

Gratitude Journal

"If you want to make peace with your enemy, you have to work with your enemy. Then he becomes your partner."

Nelson Mandela

Gratitude Journal

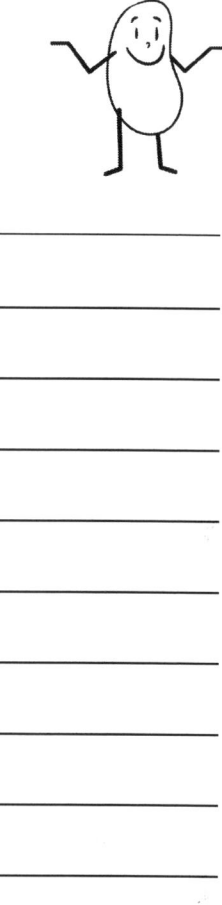

"Gratitude is the smile of love."

Ralph Marston

Gratitude Journal

> *"When you focus on gratitude the tide of disappointment goes out and the tide of love rushes in."*
>
> — *Kristin Armstrong*

Gratitude Journal

"Gratitude changes your personal vibration and how you feel inside."

Jacqueline Merne

Gratitude Journal

"Gratitude shifts your focus from what your life lacks to the abundance that is already present."

Marelisa Fábrega

Gratitude Journal

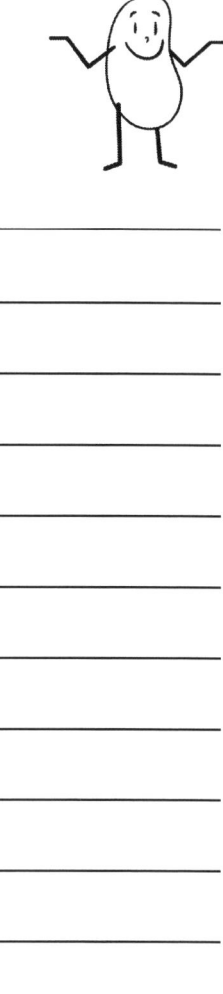

> *"He who thanks but with the lips thanks but in part, the full, the true thanksgiving comes from the heart."*
>
> *J.A. Shedd*

Gratitude Journal

> "Blessed are those that can give without remembering and receive without forgetting."
>
> Unknown

Gratitude Journal

THE HAPPY BEANS 'BEST DAY EVER' JOURNAL

"There is a calmness to a life lived in gratitude, a quite joy."

Ralph H. Blum

Gratitude Journal

> "Real life isn't always going to be perfect or go our way, but the recurring acknowledgement of what is working in our lives can help us not only to survive but surmount our difficulties."
>
> Sarah Ban Breathnach

Gratitude Journal

_____
_____
_____
_____
_____
_____
_____
_____
_____

Use this space to be creative

"Gratitude like oxygen gives us our life force."

Jacqueline Merne

Gratitude Journal

> *"Silent gratitude isn't much use to anyone."*
>
> **G.B. Stern**

Gratitude Journal

> *"Gratitude is the music of the heart when its cords are swept by the breeze of kindness."*
>
> *Author Unknown*

Gratitude Journal

"Your prayer in your distress and in your need, would that you might pray also in the fullness of your joy and in your days of abundance."

Khalil Gibran

Gratitude Journal

"Lead from the back – and let others believe they are in front."

Nelson Mandela

Gratitude Journal

"Gratitude is finding nature uplifting. Look up, see the blue skies and twinkling stars at night. Breath in the freshness of the air and reap the rewards of the simple observation."

Jacqueline Merne

Gratitude Journal

> "A man is but the product of his thoughts. What he thinks he becomes."
>
> Mahatma Gandhi

Gratitude Journal

> *"Your life is your greatest teacher."*
>
> *Oprah Winfrey*

Gratitude Journal

> *"As we express our gratitude, we must never forget that the highest appreciation is not to utter words, but to live by them."*
>
> *John F. Kennedy*

Gratitude Journal

"Happiness cannot be travelled to, owned, worn or consumed. Happiness is the spiritual experience of living every minute with love, grace and gratitude."

Denis Waitley

Gratitude Journal

_____
_____
_____
_____
_____
_____
_____
_____

Use this space to be creative

"Gratitude can transform common days into thanksgivings, turn routine jobs into joy, and change ordinary opportunities into blessings."

William Arthur Ward

Gratitude Journal

> *"Smile more, it's contagious and spreads like wildfire."*
>
> *Jacqueline Merne*

Gratitude Journal

> "Gratitude is the most exquisite form of courtesy."
>
> Jacques Maritain

Gratitude Journal

> *"It is through gratitude for the present moment that the spiritual dimension of life opens up."*
>
> *Eckhart Tolle*

Gratitude Journal

> "There are only two ways to live your life. One is as though nothing is a miracle the other is as though everything is a miracle."
>
> Albert Einstein

Gratitude Journal

> "The struggle ends when the gratitude begins."
>
> *Neale Donald Walsch*

Gratitude Journal

THE HAPPY BEANS 'BEST DAY EVER' JOURNAL

"Be thankful every day and come alive."

Jacqueline Merne

Gratitude Journal

> *"Don't worry about the years, live for the day and be happy."*
>
> *Maureen Merne (my lovely Mother)*

Gratitude Journal

Use this space to be creative

MY 3R RULE

Follow My 3R Rule

- Repeat

- Repeat

- Reap the benefits of your Personal Happy Beans Gratitude Journal.

Just keep going no matter what.

ABOUT THE AUTHOR

Jacqueline Merne, author of 'Stress To Success – The Hottest Facts & The Coolest Solutions' has an astute mind and a caring, creative nature. She is a person of integrity and uncommon empathy.

Jacqueline is uniquely suited to helping others uncover their true goals and fulfil their personal aspirations. She runs her own business in holistic wellness, stress management and resilience training. She is a strong believer in securing personal freedom in all its forms.

Jacqueline has worked in a number of war-torn and famine-stricken African countries, where she became only too aware of the necessity for managing personal wellness effectively. As Jacqueline says we all must nurture our physical and mental health equally. Each has a vital role to play in our overall personal wellness allowing us to flourish.

Jacqueline's extensive experiences in Africa and India helped cement her understanding of the magical power of gratitude. She says "To see first-hand how people who have virtually nothing at all show so much gratitude for the simplest of things has etched a place in my heart and enriched my life forever." She truly believes this has opened her eyes to a life filled with joy, happiness and true contentment.

By truly feeling gratitude in your daily life you too can overcome many obstacles and embrace positive change in your own life.

Jacqueline's mission statement is

"To be the best version of myself that I can be and to empower others to find a path to their personal success."

She supports The Hope Foundation for street children in Kolkata (Calcutta), India. Their Vision is a world where it should never hurt to be a child.'

Jacqueline lives near London with her husband, Gerry, and enjoys a fulfilling purposeful life. In her spare time she creates wall art and hand paints vintage furniture to give a shabby-chic look. She loves to practice Heartfulness meditation, finds being close to nature relaxing and regularly takes walks by the river near her home.

Jacqueline is an accomplished Speaker, Trainer, Educator and Author. She provides training in the following to individuals, businesses and other interested groups.

- Creator of Bespoke Programmes in Personal Resilience
- Programmes in Maximising Performance
- Engaging Speaker
- Creator of 'The Mind Your BEANS Programme' © for Personal Wellness

For further information on any of the above contact Jacqueline as follows

Contact Details   w   www.mindyoyurbeans.co.uk

                              e   info@mindyourbeans.co.uk

Also written by Jacqueline Merne

Printed in Great Britain
by Amazon